We're All On a Journey to Find Truth

The Life and History of Sojourner Truth
A 31 Day Devotional for Women

© **By Joyce Marrie, MA, RDT.**

hloe Publishing

Minneapolis MN

We're All On a Journey to Find Truth
The Life and History of Sojourner Truth - A 31-Day Devotional for
Women
ISBN 1-4243-0133-1

Copyright ©2007 by Joyce Marrie, MA, RDT
All rights reserved. No part of this publication may be reproduced or
transmitted in any form or by any means without written permission of
the publisher.
2nd addition revised version 2008

Published by **Chloe Publishing**
PO Box 26054
St. Louis Park, MN 55426

Edited by: Dr. Sharon Votel

Printed in the United State of America

Unless otherwise indicated, all Scriptures quotations are taken from the
King James Version of the Bible.

Dedications

Thanks to God the inspiration and wisdom he imparts to me through his word.
To my family, Anthony, Terry jr. and Joy

To my Mom, (Mildred) for your loving support and encouragement
My sister's Ruth & Lorretta, and all of my extended family... love ya

Dr. Sharon Votel my colleague and friend, for your inspiration and support

Eric & Carletta Yancy, for your support and encouragement

Ed & Regina Irwin, thanks for speaking into my life and for your words of encouragement

Mary Hamilton, for your support and encouragement

Paul Warder, Photographer

Mary Leoni, thank you so much for your support

Vicki Keck copying assistance

.
Thanks to all my family and friends
God Bless all of you!!!

3

Preface

This devotion book is a practical way for women to understand their struggle, applying life with a purpose through the word of God, finding healing, reconciliation to fulfill their purpose.

Begin to open your heart and receive an impartation of life.
Be ye transformed by the renewing of your mind. Romans 12:2

"If ye continue in my word, then are ye my disciples indeed;
And ye shall know the truth, and the truth shall make you free"
John 8:31-32, KJV

Table of Contents

Day 1

Think Back to the Beginning

In 1797, Isabella Hardenbergh is born a slave in Hurley, New York

Sojourner (Isabella) was born a slave to parents James and Elizabeth (Mau-Mau Bett)[i] Bomefree. No record was made of her birth. The name Bomefree means tree and had been given to her father who was very tall. She was the youngest of many siblings who had already been sold which made her parents afraid they would lose her too. When she was three years old Slave Master Charles Hardenbergh died. His son moved Isabella's family from their cabin to the dark and cold cellar of his house where they all got sick. Through all of the pain and loss Isabella took courage in her mother's storytelling, love, prayers, and teachings about God. She remembered always being close by, secure in a basket tied high in the branches of a tree or wrapped snugly on her mother's back while she worked, soothed by her body's rhythms. As Isabella grew older she understood her mother's stress and pain, honored her messages of faith and hope, and grew in love.

Think Today

Our beginnings stay with us throughout our lives and may influence how we raise our own children. It is important to honor and to learn from our own lives as we learn from Sojourner's life story. Mindful of our beginnings, we can move forward into our destiny.

Ask Yourself
When you think back to your childhood, what do you remember?
What were your parents like?
What pain and struggles might they have had?
Who was a strong influence in your life and why?

Biblical Passage
Before I formed you in the belly I knew you.
Jeremiah 1:5

*Please note that Sojourner had several names in her lifetime. It was not until she was an adult that she chose the name that is most familiar, Sojourner Truth. The author will refer to her as Bell throughout the majority of the book.

Time to Reflect

Day 2

Take Time to Weep

In 1806, Bell was sold to John Neely in Kingston, New York.

When Bell was nine years old, Master Hardenbergh died. She was taken from her mother and sold to the Neely's for $100 like a head of cattle. What an emotional trauma! She did not have much of a childhood, having grown up too fast from doing the back breaking work of a house slave. Before she was half grown, she had lost both parents and all of her siblings. Bell didn't know English because her early language was Dutch. In fact, she learned the *Lord's Prayer* in Dutch from her mother[ii]. Mr. Neely had no patience for her lack of understanding and Bell received her first beating because of this. Many times she had to keep quiet, holding in her pain. She later remarked that through writing, she was able to get some of those early hurts out instead of developing a slave mentality. Bell used her painful experiences as stepping-stones to a better future.

Think Today

Abuse, fear, shame, and mistrust go hand in hand. Emotions drive us and we may try to accept this by putting up a wall of denial. This can lead to mental and physical isolation and even a slave mentality (i.e., a lack of self-confidence, personal autonomy, or independent thought, belief in one's insignificance, a desire to please the powerful at any cost, and a ferocious anger turned inward that can surge into frightening outbursts)[iii]. As women, we often cover up our pain. Perhaps we think we cannot trust or perhaps our friends have turned their backs on us; whatever the reason, we do not believe anyone will understand. When we stuff those feelings, however, they will haunt us later. We must instead turn those scars into stars and reach out to others. We must ask God to bring true friends into our life, friends that will celebrate our uniqueness, pray with us, empathize with our pain, and not discredit us.

Ask Yourself

Reflect on a time when you were in an abusive situation and wanted to tell someone
but did not because you feared they would not understand
or reveal your secret to someone else.
What did you learn about yourself at this difficult moment?
How do you typically stuff your pain?

Biblical Passage

Weeping may endure for a night, but joy comes in the morning.
Psalms 30:5

Time to Reflect

_____

_____

_____

_____

_____

_____

_____

_____

_____

_____

_____

_____

_____

Day 3

Trust in Your Potential

In 1807 Bell was sold to Martin Schriver for $105.

Bell's father heard of the way she was being treated at the Neely's and asked Mr. Schriver to buy her away from them. This is where Bell started to learn English. Schriver took time to communicate with her and showed more understanding than Neely. He owned an inn and was a fisherman, so Bell sometimes did both types of work.

Think Today
Sometimes we struggle and it doesn't seem like anyone understands, just like Bell as she tried to learn English. We may ask, "Why me?" When we focus on our problems we can't see the opportunities that lie ahead. Like Bell, we can choose to have a slave mentality or tell ourselves, "I can do this" and look beyond the box of our circumstances. We only live once and every circumstance can teach us how to get better at what we're trying to accomplish. We have a picture of how things will work for us, but sometimes it does not look like it will happen. It's hard to stretch beyond the box where we are used to seeing ourselves. Women, we must not limit ourselves. We must jump out of the box to discover our true gifts and potential.

Ask Yourself
Where is your faith at this moment, inside or outside of the box?
Describe the faith picture you are visualizing. Or draw it in this journal.
If you see yourself beyond the box mentality, where is it leading you?
How are you pushing forward?

Biblical Passage
I can do all things through Christ who strengthens me.
Philippians 4:13

Day 4

Remember You Are Already Accepted by God

Bell knew her heart and spoke her truth.

Bell walked and talked with God throughout her life; whenever things weren't right she spoke up. She knew what it was like to not be accepted for her color or gender. In her *Narratives* she said, "I'm against slavery because I know what it's like to be a woman that has no rights."[iv] She didn't compromise on her stand. In the 1850's, women did not speak in public. Bell did speak because she believed that slavery should be abolished. Her simple moving speeches were honest and clear. She had a low, powerful speaking and singing voice and mixed songs and words when she appeared in public.[v] She used her communication skills to bring about change and did not allow herself to feel defeated by what people thought or the rejections she received. She knew that God accepted her.

Think Today
Women, our self-esteem is very important to us. It affects how we look, how others accept us and how we interact through actions and words. Communication takes work because we are so easily misunderstood. Our thoughts have a lot to do with what we feel and say, especially if we dwell on the negative more than the positive. We need to understand that it is very important to listen to others and ourselves before we speak. We often look on the outside and do not take time to look on the inside at the things that we really need to see. Along with holding false assumptions and wanting so badly to be liked, we must be careful not to gossip or blame others to make ourselves feel better. It is so important to share with one another in God's love regardless of whose opinion is right. We can make it right by interpreting the message with love and compassion. Only then can we move forward.

Ask Yourself
In what ways do you dwell on the negative?
How do you think you can change that?
What does your self-esteem look like? What is its source?
How much is it dependent on someone else's praise?
In what ways are you letting rejection stop you from moving ahead?
What stand are you taking, or do you stand for what is right?

Biblical Passage
So a man thinks so is he.
Proverbs 23:7

Time to Reflect

Day 5

Make Your Time Count

Bell worked hard with no time to play.

Bell had to get up early, no doubt, and help Master Shriver with his businesses from sunup to sundown. How hard it must have been to want to play like any child. Master Shriver hovered like a pesky fly that could not be shooed away.

Think Today
Everything is not given to us on a silver platter. We have to work for what we get even when it is free, for it will surely cost us in some other way down the road. Months and years pass by so quickly and we miss the opportunities amid the distractions of those pesky flies. Opportunity comes once, twice and many times more but do we take it? No. We hope; we watch for something greater. And opportunity passes us by. The first opportunity we pass up may be one's greater life calling. Women we must not waste time; waste is haste and turns into procrastination. The door to opportunity must not be ignored.

Ask Yourself
What constant distractions are keeping you from opportunity?
What opportunities have you resisted along the way and why did you resist them?
What things sap your time and have no personal benefit?

Biblical Passage
Be very careful, then, how you live not as unwise but as wise, making the most of every opportunity, because the days are evil. Therefore do not be foolish, but understand what the Lord's will is.
Ephesians 5:15-17

Time to Reflect

_____

_____

_____

_____

_____

_____

_____

_____

_____

_____

_____

_____

_____

_____

_____

Day 6

Envision Faith
Bell kept her vision of her mother's faith alive in her heart.

No doubt young Bell turned to faith when there was no understanding, as her mother had before her. Her vision of her mother praying kept her moving forward. She believed change would come through effort and that faith alone would conquer fear. She had a growing sense of purpose and knew that walking in faith gave meaning to her each and every step. She kept looking to God as her source of truth and life.

Think Today
Faith can do the unexpected. We may have a picture of how things will work out but what actually happens is totally different. Perhaps distractions have interrupted our focus to the extent that faith seems impossible. It is not God who has instilled that doubt, fear, and dimness of understanding or perception. He does things in his time and he needs no help from us, other than to hold firm in faith. Where there is no faith vision there is no purpose. Trust in the Lord and he will defeat your enemies and reveal to you your true purpose.

Ask Yourself
Describe your faith vision, now and in the future.
How has your faith vision changed over time?
How does your faith make you feel?
What is your growing sense of purpose?

Biblical Passage
If you have faith as a grain of a mustard seed you can say unto this mountain be removed. Matthew 17:20
Now faith is the substance of things hoped for. Hebrews 11:1-6

21

Time to Reflect

Study Faith

Seed Seed Grow – The Seed of Faith
Joyce Marrie

Each day I wait as I water it daily
Seed seed grow
The storms came and the winds blow
Seed seed grow
Each day I wait as I water it daily
Seed seed grow
As the sun beats down
Seed seed grow
I don't think it's in the ground
Seed seed grow
It's cold......Oh why is it so slow
Seed seed grow
Listen....patience......patience.....my child
Keep watering it daily
Seed seed grow....................

Day 7

Forgive and Forget

Bell practiced self-sacrifice and forgiveness.

Bell suffered much throughout her life, from being called a witch to being blamed for situations beyond her control. As a child, she forgave the masters who beat her even when she did not understand why she was being beaten. Some of those beatings were so brutal that her back bled and she carried scars for life.

Think Today
Women, not forgiving can hold us back. Don't be dismayed over the negative words that are spoken because God believes in us and his words are life. Recognize Jesus helps us through our pain? Through his pain and suffering. Forgive and forget; it's a phrase we hear many times. It's so difficult to forget when we've been hurt by someone or we are suffering for what is right. It's easier to engage in gossip and succumb to spiritual warfare. Looking beyond the pain inflicted by others can give us strength and healing, in our own way and time. It's very difficult to do this, but we must be willing to hold fast no matter how others perceive it. Doing the right thing is painful but in the long run, it helps us build character and integrity.

Ask Yourself
Describe a time when you forgave someone.
How were you able to put the situation behind you?
When do you hold grudges?

Biblical Passage
If you do not forgive, neither will your heavenly Father forgive you.
Matthew 2:26

Time to Reflect

_____

_____

_____

_____

_____

_____

_____

_____

_____

_____

_____

_____

_____

_____

_____

Day 8

Grow Strong in God's Eyes

In 1810, Bell was sold for $175 to John Dumont of New Paltz, New York.

A new home, master, family, and workload were more challenges than one person can handle. Bell was now 13 and had the strength of an adult. Mr. Dumont was proud of his purchase and expected his profits to increase as Bell matured and had children of her own. Adolescent Bell had her own hopes and dreams, one of which was to do anything it took to gain freedom. Bell later said she looked upon Dumont as "a God."[vi] She was very attached to this family since she was with them longer than she had been with her parents. However, she suffered both physical and sexual abuse during those years, as did many slaves.[vii]

Think Today
Sometimes we just need to bide our time and grow in strength and resolve. God waits; he knows development is a long and steady process. As adolescents, we take a look at the pieces of ourselves and weave them into a stronger whole. We look forward to a future as an adult in society. We are hopeful that what is ahead is better than what came before. Life is a journey. We carry with us our lessons from the past and our hopes for the future. We grow stronger in God's eyes.

Ask Yourself
What lessons from the past do you carry forward?
How have your life's experiences shaped you?
In what ways are you now stronger in the eyes of God?
What hopes do you have for the future?

Biblical Passage

Take my yoke upon you and learn from me, for I am gentle and humble
in heart,
and you will find rest for your souls.
For my yoke is easy and my burden is light.
Matthew 11:29&30

Time to Reflect

Day 9

Trust in a Better Tomorrow

Bell spent 16 years as John Dumont's slave.

Bell spent a lot of her growing-up years as John Dumont's slave. She was married off to one of his slaves and had babies at their birth all of her children became Dumont's property. The word got out that New York slaves would soon be granted freedom, so Bell approached Master Dumont, asking him if he would consider freeing her a year early. As her part of the bargain she would work harder than before. They struck a deal and she happily held his promise in her heart. She worked so hard she hurt her hand, permanently damaging her fingers. When the time finally arrived for her to be free, however, Mr. Dumont didn't say a word. "What does this mean?" Bell might have pondered, "Did he forget? Did he lie? Did he change his mind?" She again faced him and reminded him of his promise. He betrayed her, telling her there was no deal and to leave him alone.

Think Today
Trust is a great obligation. Many times we don't trust; we fear the unknown or we have been betrayed before. Not everyone makes good on his or her promises. When making a promise, a good thing to keep in mind or say is, "If it's the Lord's will, I will do it." If we have broken promises to others we may not always be able to go back, but we can make a fresh start today.

Ask Yourself
Who have you promised something to and not kept that promise?
What was the nature of that promise?
What has been standing in your way?

Biblical Passage

It is better not to vow than to make a vow and not fulfill it.
Ecclesiastes 5:5

If the Lords will. James 4:15

Time to Reflect

_____

_____

_____

_____

_____

_____

_____

_____

_____

_____

_____

Day 10

Treat Others with Honesty

Bell stood up to Master Dumont when he refused to free her.

Bell's master broke his vow to free her. She confronted him and it was not a good feeling to have to go and speak up for what was right. But she did it and he rejected her. His mouth spoke one thing and his heart spoke another. We tend to think that saying one thing and meaning something else in our heart will solve the problem, but it doesn't. Bell, depending on God who gave her strength, knew her purpose. Truth was important to her, but she had not always been honored or supported by those around her. There were many times in which she had to stand alone.

Think Today

How many of us depend on other people? There does come a time when we have to stand alone and through this, we learn to grow. Honesty starts in the heart. An honest person will go a long way in life. Many times we hide the truth of how we really feel and go on in life with a grudge or false truth. We need to let others know the truth about ourselves and deal with it. Why are we so afraid to be honest? Is it because of rejection or fear? It is so easy to hide behind our fears and cover up the very thing that will help others to break free of their insecurities. It is painful when someone is not honest especially when there is also rejection. We must give the painful feelings to God and allow him to work through us and keep a forgiving heart. We must use this as an opportunity to grow. There is a bigger picture. The next time around we will have gained wisdom on how to deal with dishonesty. We must be willing to confront when situations arise and maintain our true heart.

Ask Yourself

What does honesty mean to you?

Think of a time you were honest despite fearing the consequences; what did you learn about yourself? When it is hard for you to be honest, what is it that you fear?

Biblical Passage

He that is faithful in that which is least is faithful also in much: and he that is unjust in the least is unjust also in much.

Luke 16:10

Time to Reflect

_____

_____

_____

_____

_____

_____

_____

_____

_____

_____

_____

Make the Best of a Bad Situation

Bell married Thomas, a fellow slave.

Bell loved Robert who was owned by another master but Dumont had already married her to one of his slave hands, Thomas, who was much older than she. Bell and Robert would sneak and see each other until Master Dumont found out and had Robert beaten and ordered not to see her again. Bell and Thomas had children and did the best they could as parents. Dumont promised them a cottage of their own after they were emancipated under state law in 1827 and they planned to continue to live together. Bell's life didn't stop when she couldn't stay with Robert. She made a life with Thomas, knowing she had a bigger purpose.

Think Today

Making the best of a bad situation is a good thing. It is healthy to turn the bad or negative situation around. We will not have fulfillment in life without a purpose.

Ask Yourself

Reflect on a current situation that could be better.
How are you making the best of it?
What do you hope will happen in the long run?

Biblical Passage

They that sow in tears shall reap in joy.
Psalms 126:5

Time to Reflect

_____

_____

_____

_____

_____

_____

_____

_____

_____

_____

_____

_____

Day 12

Keep on Asking, "Where Are Our Children Today?"

Bell had five children, one of whom died in infancy.

Bell saw her children become Master Dumont's property and sold off into slavery. While they were little, however, she raised them lovingly and well. Her son Peter was sold at age five or six to an in-law so Bell relied on God to get him back, declaring, "I'll have my child again!"[viii] She later said, "So tall within—I felt as if the power of a nation was within me."[ix] With the help of her community, good advice, and many legal fees, Bell filed a complaint with the grand jury and after a year, prevailed. She was the first African American to win a lawsuit. Peter was traumatized from his separation and maltreatment and had developed a slave mentality. Bell had to convince him she was his mother and would stick with him from that point on. Peter later got caught stealing and continued to get into trouble despite her loving support and that of the community. Even in Bell's time, the saying, "It takes a village to raise a child" held true.

Think Today

Where are our children today?

Too many are being raised by the media and it is corrupting their minds. On some level we all have allowed it to happen and the effect is as harmful as the slave mentality of Sojourner's time. How can our children find their identity, seek their purpose of being, and discover their God-given creativity in today's world of enslavement to warped imaginations and false value systems. Cars, appearance, money; it boils down to a materialistic, ego-centered generation, looking out for Number One. And what is the cost? A life with hopes and dreams replaced with personal material gain. Today many parents do not know where their children are. Some children are even abandoned while parents support drug habits. Most children go to school, but what do they have to come home to? The streets are their repose. This was unheard of in Sojourner's time. Our children and our neighbors' children count on us as part of that village. We adults are part of the fabric of our children's memories, and in turn, have a very real impact on their future. We must free our children from the negative influences that surround them, and support them with faith and love.

Ask Yourself
What can you say or do about the slave mentality of our young people today?
Why is it so important to shift from an I-centered to a we-centered perspective?
What is a favorite memory about your parents?
What do you want your children or young acquaintances to remember about you?

Biblical Passage
Suffer the little children to come unto me, and forbid them not: for such is the kingdom of God.
Mark 10:13-14

Time to Reflect

Day 13

Don't Let People Pleasers Detract You from Your Purpose

Bell remained true to her calling.

Despite events in Bell's life not always being what she wanted, she was not a people-pleaser and would not allow her masters to get in the way of her decision to run and make something of herself. Where would she be today if she had not stepped out and followed her calling? She was focused; she saw a bigger picture through the eyes of faith.

Think Today

Sometimes we are more willing to please others than to please ourselves. It's not wrong to help others but we must ask, "Am I helping myself at the same time?" Why do we try so hard to please others? Perhaps we don't want to appear to hurt anyone or we want people to like us. There are so many things in life that we want to do but the questions remain: "What is the motive behind this?" "Is this going in the direction that I'm headed?" We must not put our focus on people but on God. He is the master, chief builder, author, and finisher of our faith. People-pleasers take us away from our dreams and aspirations. We all need to learn the word "No."

Ask Yourself

Think of a time when you sought to please others rather than to please God.

What was your motivation?

In what ways are you living a fulfilled life with your dreams and aspirations?

What work do you yet have to do?

38

Biblical Passage

And whatever you do, do it heartily, as to the Lord and not to men, knowing that from the Lord you will receive the reward of the inheritance; for you serve the Lord Christ.

Colossians 3:22-24

Time to Reflect

Day 14

Resolutely Step through Fear for You Are Valuable

In 1826, Bell walked with her baby, Sophia, to freedom. Bell was afraid of the dark so she prayed to God and he showed her what to do. She then stepped out to freedom. She left a little before dawn, one arm around her baby and the other around a handkerchief sack with meager food and clothes. As she wearily stopped to rest, doubts rose up and she might have said: "Oh where am I going?" "What do I think I'm doing to leave behind a sure thing?" Then she prayed again to God for directions. As Bell kept stepping forward, she began to see the light. She was led to the Van Wagenen's home where they showed her the love of God. They paid Dumont his asking price of $20 for Bell and $5 for Sophia so he would not try to claim them[x]. Bell and Sophia stayed with the family for a year and even adopted their name. Bell's faith grew stronger and bolder.

Think Today
Many times we are halted by what we see in our past and our fear prevents us from moving ahead. This is just like babies taking a first step, falling, and hesitating to get back up again. We need to continue to seek God in those times of uncertainty and he will guide us. Fear is one of the main barriers to freedom. A lot of mistakes are made in fear such as killing, sickness, and even death. Fear grips our imagination and keeps us in bondage if we let it. Women we must step into our destiny. The more steps we take, the less the fear prevails.

Ask Yourself
What fears typically hold you back?
Reflect on a situation in which you moved forward despite your fear.
How did you do it?
What steps are you taking to freedom?

Biblical Passage

For God has not given us a spirit of fear, but of power, and love, and a sound mind.

2 Timothy 1:7

Time to Reflect

_____

_____

_____

_____

_____

_____

_____

_____

_____

_____

_____

Day 15

Break Through Your Mind's Shackles

Bell was legally freed on July 4, 1827, as a result of a New York statute.

Bell was a woman who could relate to name-calling and physical abuse but that didn't stop her from fulfilling her purpose in life. She knew her calling and was determined to fulfill it, no matter what it cost her. She inspired all women to fight back and to use the right tools. God was on her side and in her heart. By now Bell could claim three types of freedom. First, she left Dumont when she thought the time was right. Second, she replaced her fear with God's love. And third, empowered by her faith, she broke out of slavery's passivity and used the law to achieve her freedom.[xi]

Think Today
As women, do we feel we're not respected and that enough is enough? Has our self-image been devalued through the negative attitudes, actions, and hurtful words of others? We've taken all we can take and will accept no more! We are unique, special, and loved by someone who cares more than we can ever comprehend. God says, "I have loved you with an everlasting love" that no human can give. We must get up and listen to God. He's called us not to empathize with our misfortune, but to celebrate our value, both inside and out. We must see ourselves as beautiful and valuable in God's eyes.

Ask Yourself
Who do you surround yourself with?
In what ways do others make you feel loved and valued?
In what ways do you feel worthless and abused?
What are you going to do to break through your mind's shackles and shine?

Biblical Passage

Whatsoever things are true, whatsoever things are honest, whatsoever things are just, whatsoever things are pure, whatsoever things are lovely, whatsoever things are of good report; if there be any virtue, and if there be any praise, think on these things.

Philippians 4:8

Time to Reflect

_____

_____

_____

_____

_____

_____

_____

_____

_____

_____

_____

Day 16
Claim Your Freedom

In 1829, Bell moved in with her son, Peter, in New York City.

Escape doesn't always come easily because of life's challenges and battles, many of which take place in the mind. Even legally free and able to live independently with her son, it would have taken Bell awhile to feel free of the real shackles, chains, whips, broken promises, oppression, name-calling, and the slave mentality this treatment could produce. When freedom came so close that she could taste it and then was denied, she felt angry and betrayed. Then she took a pause until she could see freedom in her thoughts through faith. She might have spoken out, "I want to be free and I want others to be free!" and then she acted on what she saw. Each step she took freed her physically and psychologically from the shackles of a slave mentality.

Think Today
The mind is the most powerful source of our body's wisdom. What we feed our mind and how we use it determines our mental, spiritual, physical, and social freedom. This freedom is also based on the choices we make. Whether positive or negative, the outcome is evident. Free our bodies and our thoughts in God's grace and our actions will follow.

Ask Yourself
In a perfect world, what would freedom look like to you?
Describe a time when you were held in bondage.
How did you resolve it, by your emotions or God's grace?
What is shackling your mind and body?
What steps are you taking to freedom?

Biblical Passage
Casting down imaginations, and every high thing that exalted itself

45

against the knowledge of God, and bringing into captivity every thought to the obedience of Christ.

2 Corinthians 10:5

Time to Reflect

_____

_____

_____

_____

_____

_____

_____

_____

_____

_____

Day 17
Make Your Word Your Bond

While working as a maid, Bell trained to be a preacher.

Once in New York, Bell worked as a maid. Surviving was hard. She was a single parent and Peter's behavior was difficult[xii] but she remained focused on her goals. She wanted to preach, to show others how to talk with God, to make the world a better place. It is said that Bell had a vision. She recalled running into Dumont one day after moving in with the Van Wagenen family and seeing a light beaming "with the beauty of holiness and radiant with love."[xiii] She believed she was baptized by the Holy Spirit and from that point on had Jesus as a friend, a "soul-protecting fortress."[xiv] She started out by preaching with friends in camp meetings around the city. She had a great memory and knew Bible verses by heart, for she had never learned to read. She would ask others to read Bible passages to her and her knowledge grew. At age 40, Bell felt ready to preach, making her words her bonds.

Think Today
If promises remain unfulfilled they become lies. This affects everyone involved and the person making the promises is no longer seen as trustworthy. The broken promises become another form of bondage. The results may include confusion, anger, fear, wounded pride, backstabbing, and deception. We must free ourselves of any lies that keep us in bondage. We must tell the truth no matter how tempting it is to lie.

Ask Yourself
Reflect on a time when you broke your promise to a loved one.
How did you feel, then and later on?
What did you learn from this?

Biblical Passage
You shall know the truth and the truth shall make you free.

John 8:32
Speak the truth in Love Ephesians 4:15

Time to Reflect

_____

_____

_____

_____

_____

_____

_____

_____

_____

_____

Day 18
Say What You Mean and Mean What You Say

Bell began to speak her thoughts.

Bell had a presence about her that came across to others as intimidating, strong, and overpowering. It was said that the impact of her preaching was "miraculous," that "even learned and respectable people were running after her,"[xv] and that she "out prayed and out preached her compeers."[xvi] She was a tall woman who walked and spoke with such confidence that many didn't know how to take her. They missed the heart of her true character. Some people outright opposed her, which made communicating very difficult.

Think Today
Being misunderstood is frustrating and many doubts can arise. Is the misunderstanding due to poor word choices or the speaker's emotion, accent, or voice tone? Is it due to the listener's resistance to accepting what was said? In these situations, we must realize that we cannot fight the battle alone. We have to rely on God. We must learn to let go and not get caught up in the listener's statements or actions. We must back off and give that person room to grow.

Our bodies have many ways to communicate, positively as well as negatively. Our actions may speak much more loudly than our words.

Ask Yourself
How do you typically express yourself to others?
In what circumstances does it feel more difficult to be understood?
At these times, how do you bring clarity to what you're trying to get across?

Biblical Passage
In all thy getting get understanding.
In all thy ways acknowledge Him and he shall direct thy path.
Proverbs 3:6

Time to Reflect

_____

_____

_____

_____

_____

_____

_____

_____

_____

_____

Day 19
Make Time Count

In June of 1843 Bell changed her name to Sojourner Truth
and became a traveling preacher.

Sojourner must have thought she had no time to waste; her calling was to spread God's truth and reduce the suffering of her people. She was not comfortable living in the "great drama"[xvii] of New York City and in her *Narratives* called it "one great system of robbery and wrong."[xviii] She also felt guilty she was living more comfortably than most other people and was ready to leave, to flee "a wicked city."[xix] She went east of New York City, where the Spirit called her. She made every minute count and today, although little is written, her actions took root and bloomed. She is truly an inspiration.

Think Today
Often, the risks we take are costly for they rob us of valuable time. Time wasted is time lost, and these setbacks may result in personal stagnation or loss of vision. Wise use of time has both present and future benefits. Ultimately, life is how we spend our time and timing is everything when it comes to success. Time is of the essence. In life, time has its costs; we can pay now or we pay later.

Ask Yourself
What is your sense of the passing of time at this point in your life?
What do you still want to accomplish?
What do you value in life?
How does what you value add or waste time?
In what circumstances are you stuck in time?

Biblical Passage
Be not one as beating the air.

1 Corinthians 9:26
Redeem the time Ephesians 5:16

Time to Reflect

_____

_____

_____

_____

_____

_____

_____

_____

_____

_____

Day 20
When God Speaks, Listen

In 1850, Sojourner began to speak out against slavery and to champion
women's rights.

Sojourner Truth picked a good name for herself. A sojourner moves
around from place to place and truth is what preachers speak.^{xx} She
spoke but not everyone listened. She was frequently attacked by mobs of
angry people yielding sticks and rocks, seeking to destroy both her and
her messages of truth. One time as she fearfully hid behind a tree trunk
hoping the mob would go away, she heard the voice of the Lord and his
message of mercy. Had she given into her fears, she might have died.
But she gave herself fully to his message and went right back preaching.
She was very aware that time was passing and that she must act quickly.

Think Today
Many opportunities are missed when people do not stop and listen. Time
is of the essence in really hearing what is said. When God speaks, he
may use words, people, and anything in creation to get his message
across. We must listen to that still voice in our hearts as God knocks and
waits for us to open the door.

Ask Yourself
What messages do you get from your inner voice?
Reflect on times you make hasty decisions without listening first.
What opportunities have you missed?
Describe a situation in which you believed you were listening to God.
When God speaks, what voice do you hear?

Biblical Passage
Hearken unto my voice. Mark 7:14
Isaiah 51:1

Time to Reflect

_____

_____

_____

_____

_____

_____

_____

_____

_____

_____

Day 21
Judge Not

Sojourner spread her message with wisdom and conviction. Sojourner was judged for whom she was, a black confident woman. She did not walk with her head down and folks found that intimidating. She was frequently despised for both her race and gender. She didn't follow the crowd; more often the crowed followed her. Sojourner fought for what we take for granted today. She had an attitude, the right kind of attitude. She meant business. She didn't go around talking about her sisters and brothers. She was an ordinary person with a powerful calling. She told her story as a way to help others. She knew her calling and her pulpit and understood she would be accepted by some and rejected by others. She also knew the Bible regardless of her illiteracy. God still used her; isn't that amazing?

Think Today
Today we have a different attitude about our sisters and brothers and we use words to destroy one another. We fail to celebrate differences and do not understand that we can go a lot further in life if we put the past behind and stop judging one another. Would Sojourner's message have prevailed had she given into people calling her illiterate, ignorant, or ugly? The Apostle Peter was considered unlearned and peculiar. He had no schooling and yet God used him and his story at a time when the people with great education lacked the faith to believe in the impossible. We must remember God works through ordinary people. Every one of us has a story to tell. We must open our hearts and check ourselves for the judge stands at the door.

Ask Yourself
Describe a time when you judged someone based on what others had said.
Who poisoned your mind?

Has someone ever judged you; how did it feel?
Do you typically judge a person on outward appearances or do you try
getting to know them first? Why?

Biblical Passage
Judge not, that ye be not judged. For with what judgment ye judge, ye
shall be judged: and with what measure ye mete, it shall be measured to
you again .

Matthew 7:1& 2

Time to Reflect

_____

_____

_____

_____

_____

_____

_____

_____

_____

_____

Day 22

Accept Yourself for You Are Already Accepted by God

Sojourner traveled far and wide.

In 1848 Sojourner was encouraged by Olive Gilbert (an early feminist and member of the Northampton Association) to write her story. Sojourner thus gave her input to the first Women's Rights Movement and attended a Women's Rights convention on July 19 and 20 in Seneca Falls, New York. Only Sojourner, with the help of God, could make herself shine brightly while communicating both to her masters and to large crowds of people. When she spoke at the convention, the wife of an old slave master, even in her hesitation, could do nothing but to give her that respect. Sojourner resolutely walked to the front of the crowd and said, "May I speak?" She took off her bonnet and folded it. When everyone else cried out, "Don't let her speak!" she said, "Women, you don't have to worry 'bout God booing at you. He's for you and not against you."[xxi]

Think Today

If no one else celebrates us God will do so, giving us favor beyond anyone's comprehension. Rest certain in "the favor of the Lord." We must not allow ourselves to feel rejected. God accepts us and celebrates us! And He has the final say.

Ask Yourself

When rejected, what are your thoughts and what actions do you take? Do you isolate, do you wait for the praise of others, or do you trust God? How are you letting rejection keep you from your purpose?

Biblical Passage

No weapon that is formed against you will prosper and every tongue that accuses you in judgment you will condemn.
Isaiah 54:17

Time to Reflect

Day 23
Celebrate Your Worth!

In 1850 William Lloyd Garrison published Sojourner's life story,
The Narrative of Sojourner Truth.

Others also believed in Sojourner's narratives; they thought she had a message that would help in the growing number of anti-slavery protests. Sojourner was invited to have her narratives published. She replied to this offer with the comment, "Wait on the Lord and He will open doors that no man can shut."[xxii] Sojourner looked and saw the many struggles in her life, along with those of women seeking equal rights. She believed those rights were worth fighting for. Even though she was not, at this point well known, William Lloyd Garrison recognized her worth and was willing to take a risk with her.

Think Today
In life we women sometimes may wonder, are we valued or celebrated for our worth? Are we valued to the extent that God sees us? If we don't have a certain status, or measure up to some level of our perception, thank God. We are beyond value in his sight.
Women we have gifts and dreams inside of us. We must lay down our lives and let God celebrate us!

Ask Yourself
What capacities do you have to fulfill your life's purpose?
How do you know that someone is waiting for you on the other side?
Are you utilizing your God given gifts?
What is your story?

Biblical Passage
For we are his workmanship, created in Christ Jesus unto good works,

which God hath before ordained that we should walk in them.
Ephesians 2:10
He that begun a good work in you will perform it. Philippians 1:6

Time to Reflect

_____

_____

_____

_____

_____

_____

_____

_____

_____

_____

Day 24
Make Confidence Your Way of Life: You Are Somebody

In 1851, Sojourner made her famous *"Ain't I A Woman?"* speech in
Akron, Ohio

This speech has gone down in history as one of the most famous
speeches ever made. In doing so, Sojourner came to grips with her situation and took a stand.
To paraphrase, she said, "I'm unique and let my uniqueness rub off on
you; what you see is what you get. I have just as much to offer and I'm
entitled to a fair living just as anyone else." She took action and spoke
out for what she believed in. From this point on, her boldness and self-
confidence were seen as gifts, tools she could use for the betterment of
all.

Think Today
Many times we women put on a false front, due to fear of rejection or
lack of confidence. We treat ourselves as less than we are and the result
is that we take on someone else's purpose or way of doing things. We
must remember that we are unique and a perfect fit for others in their
uniqueness. We are beautifully designed in the way God intended.
Others need our confidence, but may miss the opportunity to connect
with us if we put forth false perceptions and engage in ineffective
behavior. We are somebody, unique among others and valuable in
God's eyes. We must celebrate that uniqueness!

Ask Yourself
Who are you and what are you becoming?
List 10 words that best describe how others see you.

When was the last time you took a look at yourself and asked the question, "Who am I?" Do others know who you are?

Biblical Passage
Confidence in a broken tooth is like a socket out of joint.
Proverbs 25:19
So do not throw away your confidence.
Hebrews 10: 35

Time to Reflect

_____

_____

_____

_____

_____

_____

_____

_____

_____

_____

Day 25

Build Healthy Relationships

In 1852, Sojourner gave her famous speech to Frederick Douglass: *Is God Dead?*

Sojourner had many good relationships in her time. She was willing to take risks and establish empowering connections. She had reached a zenith in her life and was comfortable in her skin. One relationship was with Frederick Douglass, a powerful abolitionist. She could be herself, straightforward in her communications with him, despite the times they didn't agree. He didn't see her any differently than a real sister who was fighting for a good cause. Sojourner did not let her past stop her from communicating and spoke the truth no matter what. One time she attended a meeting and while Frederick Douglass spoke in Faneuil Hall, Boston, she boldly asked Frederick Douglass the question, "Is God Dead?"[xxiii] and her reply became famous.

Think Today
Relationship building takes time, commitment, understanding, and patience. It just doesn't happen overnight. The secret is to establish a strong vertical relationship with God the Father. Only then is it possible to expand horizontally and develop healthy positive relationships. Love must be sincere. We must be devoted to one another in brotherly (sisterly) love.

Ask Yourself
How do your relationships with others allow you to be real without condemnation?
How do you handle unexpected information within your relationships?
Reflect on a relationship that was transformed by unanticipated news.

Biblical Passage

Let love be without dissimulation. Abhor that which is evil; cleave to that which is good.
Be kindly affectionate one to another with brotherly love; in honor preferring one another;
Honor one another above yourselves.
Romans 12:9-10

Time to Reflect

_____

_____

_____

_____

_____

_____

_____

_____

_____

_____

Day 26

Do Not Let Yourself Be Offended

In 1857, Sojourner bought a home near Battle Creek, Michigan.

Sojourner was judged by the color of her skin and by her character. She was not considered to fit in and when she spoke, some joked about it. When she was about to make her *Ain't I a Woman* speech, people demeaned her person, her message, and her attitude—until she spoke. In response to her message, her commanding voice, and her eloquence, everyone cheered.[xxiv]

Think Today

Without information, there is no understanding. People are intimidated by what they do not understand. They do not want the person bearing the intimidating message to succeed. They may hurl offenses at the speaker. What do we do at these times, particularly if we are the bearers of that message? How do we handle those who demean us? Our human nature is to protect ourselves, or as the Star Trek captain would say, "Shields up!" We must not let the threat stop us. We must instead go to that person and use communication and authentic listening to achieve understanding. We must be willing to listen without judging and wanting that person to conform to our way, which is control. If they don't understand, we must give it time and respect. Being offended can bring anger, setbacks, and keep us away from life's prosperity and blessings.

Ask Yourself

How do you typically deal with offenses?
Think about a person you have offended; how did you make it right with him or her?
How does retaliation make you feel?

Biblical Passage

And whoever shall offend one of these little ones that believe in me,
it is better for him that a millstone were hanged about his neck
and he were cast into the sea.

Mark 9:42

Time to Reflect

_____

_____

_____

_____

_____

_____

_____

_____

_____

_____

Day 27
Think Good Thoughts

In 1864, Sojourner went to Washington, DC where she helped freed slaves
and met President Abraham Lincoln.

Sojourner never forgot God; she made his thoughts hers and spread the word. She trusted that when she went down an uncharted road, God would be there. She would not have written the *Narratives* if she didn't believe that she could do it. Nor would she have spoken up for what she believed or given voice to the freed slaves' pain. Sojourner was forthright and her expressions unanticipated when she came in contact with great men. To Abraham Lincoln she declared, "Mr. Lincoln, I never heard tell of you before they put you up for president." He smiled and answered, "But I had heard of you many times before that."[xxv] She also told him she had first feared for his life, comparing him to Daniel in the lion's den, but then came to believe that God had saved him. Lincoln signed her book, "For Auntie Sojourner Truth."[xxvi] Obviously, to get this close to a famous president took good thoughts; Sojourner had to believe nothing would stop her. And her thoughts became a reality.

Think Today
Many times, when faced with opposition it seems like there is no end in sight. Our thoughts become the fear that pushes us further back into the darkness, where there is no room for a creative, unanticipated response. What we say is often built on what we think and ideas are born of good thoughts. These thoughts, along with will and emotion, determine our actions. We must learn to take control of our thoughts. We must ask, "Why am I feeling this way?" It could be that our thoughts are not lining up. We must think of ourselves today as favorable and creative persons and our ideas will flow.

Ask Yourself
Reflect on a situation in which positive thoughts resulted in positive outcomes.
How do you take control of negative thinking?
What are the benefits of this approach?

Biblical Passage
Whatsoever things are true, whatsoever things are honest, whatsoever things are just, whatsoever things are pure, whatsoever things are lovely, whatsoever things are of good report; if there be any virtue, and if there be any praise, think on these things.
Philippians 4:8
Casting down every imagination. 1Corinthians 10:4-6

Time to Reflect

_____

_____

_____

_____

_____

_____

_____

_____

_____

Day 28

Talk and Hold Fast to Your Vision

In 1865, Sojourner forced horse cars in Washington, D.C. to stop for
black passengers.

When Sojourner made her speeches, she didn't just talk, she listened.
She made mental notes about what people said and questioned her
misunderstandings. For example, in response to the efforts of feminists
to be treated equally she said, "Sisters, I'm not clear what you be after.
If women want any rights more than they've got, why don't they just take
them and not be talking about it?"[xxvii] And she practiced what she
preached. For example, in Washington, D.C., horse cars would not stop
for black passengers. So Sojourner would run after the cars and yell at
the drivers until they would stop. Soon everyone was riding, which must
have made her very happy.

Think Today
Many times we women talk a good deal, but fail to put actions to our
words. We must stop talking about would haves and should haves. We
must get up and declare our dreams and visions. We must do the
impossible and take risks. Without vision, perseverance, advocacy, and
sometimes even agitation, we will perish.

Ask Yourself
What dreams, visions or aspirations are lying dormant and need to be
resurrected?
Describe your vision for yourself in the future.
What must you do to get there?

Biblical Passage
Where there is no vision, the people perish.
Proverbs 29:18

Name your Goals

_____

_____

_____

_____

_____

_____

_____

_____

_____

_____

_____

Day 29
Have No Regrets

In 1879, Sojourner traveled to Kansas to help former southern slaves begin new lives.

Once Sojourner began her preaching, she traveled far and wide. Being a sojourner meant that she did not remain at her home. Having a home had been a lifelong dream only recently achieved with the sales of her *Narratives*.[xxviii] Many newly freed slaves also needed know-how to find homes and Sojourner put her own dreams to stay home on hold in helping them do so. She did so with no regrets.

Think Today
We must tell ourselves that all dreams are possible and go on, without regrets about the past, to achieve them. Hope is a creative thing for it helps us use our hard won wisdom to make the life we dream about. Our ultimate success requires our entry into God's time and our belief that good things can happen. We must take time to reflect on what life has taught us, without regrets, in order to move forward with hope.

Ask Yourself
Try to think of one regret that has helped to move you forward.
What legacy will you be leaving to your loved ones?
In what ways is your life as you hoped it to be?
What is your purpose for living?

Biblical Passage
For we know all things work together for the good.
Romans 8:28
He who began a good work in you. Philippians 1:6

Time to Reflect

Day 30
Find People You Can Trust and Call Your Friends

In 1870 Sojourner met President Grant.

Many times Sojourner found herself with the question, "Whom Can You Trust?" In her travels to spread God's word, it must have been difficult to make lifelong and trustworthy friends. She did make connections with great historical figures such as Abraham Lincoln, Andrew Johnson, Frederick Douglass, and Ulysses Grant. But connections do not always lead to trust or to friendship. The odds are that Sojourner led quite a lonely life and had to trust mostly in God and in herself.

Think Today
We need friends to confide in. We need friends who can reflect back our hopes, challenges, and accomplishments. We need friends who stay with us through thick and thin. In today's fast-paced world, it is harder than ever to make and maintain friends. We can confidently turn our trust to God, our ever-present friend. We must see God as he sees us from the vantage point of friend.

Ask Yourself
Reflect on your friends. What good qualities do they see in you?
Why do they remain your friends?
Why have you lost friends along the way?
What do you have to offer future friends?

Biblical Passage
I will never leave you nor forsake you.
Hebrews 13:5
You are my friends. St. John 15: 14

Time to Reflect

Day 31
Continue to Fulfill your Purpose

On November 26, 1883 Sojourner Truth died at her home in Battle Creek, Michigan. Sojourner outlived all of her children. The Civil War was over in 1865, but African Americans were still trying to free themselves from the physical and psychological scars of slavery. Women's right to vote would not be achieved until 1920, and race and gender inequality would continue. Her life, however, was not lived in vain. Through ongoing self-sacrifice, preaching, and forgiveness, Sojourner accomplished her mission to spread God's truth, to tell her story, and to lead the way toward freedom. Her dying words were, "Be a follower of the Lord Jesus."[xxix]

Think Today
Many times in life we are challenged to take a step of faith and because it may not be society's norm we back away from our vision. It is then lost until someone else picks it up and runs with it. When we believe in something we have to hold fast until the finish. When we dream, we are hoping that someday this dream will come true. Why not now? We all have gifts just waiting to be recognized and tapped into. This is our purpose for being. We were created with a purpose and that purpose must be fulfilled in this life. We can achieve this by tapping into God, for he is the source of our creative power.

Ask Yourself
What is God's purpose for you?
What creative gifts can you use to achieve your purpose?
How can Sojourner's life and message help you achieve your purpose?

Biblical Passage
But seek ye first the Kingdom of God,
and His righteousness;
and all these things shall be added unto you.

Matthew 6:33

PURPOSE/DESTINY

Bibliography

Painter, Nell Irvin. (1997). *Sojourner Truth: A Life, A Symbol*. New York: Norton.

Endnotes

i	Painter p. 11
ii	Painter, p. 13
iii	Painter, p. 17
iv	Painter, p 232
v	Painter, p. 3
vi	Painter, p. 14?
vii	Painter, pp. 14-15
viii	Painter, p. 33
ix	Painter, p. 33
x	Painter, p. 33
xi	Painter, p. 22
xii	Painter, p. 67
xiii	Painter, p. 30
xiv	Painter, p. 30
xv	Painter. pp. 43-44
xvi	Painter, p. 44
xvii	Painter, p. 73
xviii	Painter, p. 73
xix	Painter, p. 73
xx	Painter, pp. 75-76
xxi	Painter, p.167
xxii	
xxiii	Painter, p. 169
xxiv	Painter, p. 168
xxv	Painter, pp. 205-206
xxvi	Painter, pp. 205-206
xxvii	Painter, p. 169
xxviii	Painter, p. 75
xxix	Painter, p. 254

STUDY NOTES

STUDY NOTES

STUDY NOTES

STUDY NOTES